THE TIME WE HAVE MISSPENT

100 SONNETS BY
M.Z. RIBALOW

NeoPoiesisPress.com

ℛ

NeoPoesis Press, LLC
P.O. Box 38037
Houston, TX 77238-8037

NeoPoiesesPress.com

Cover, design and typography: Milo Duffin and Stephen Roxborough

M.Z. Ribalow – The Time We Have Misspent
ISBN 978-0-9855577-0-6 (paperback : alk. paper)
    1. Poetry. I. Ribalow, M.Z.

Printed in the United States of America

First Edition

For Patricia, Dasha, Sam, Rhona and Other Dark Ladies

with thanks, and deep appreciation
for encouragement and feedback,

to Bonnet, Glen, Ellen, Lucia, Spencer, Allie,
Ally, Matthew, Peter, Mark, Hilary, Shosh, Shaiel,
Daleth, Lynn, Jenna, Annie, Ann, LSC,
and the one and only Dale of the pens,
among other splendid teammates

CONTENTS

Wʜᴀᴛ Lɪꜰᴇ Rᴇᴀʟʟʏ Mᴇᴀɴᴛ

If images that flicker through my mind
in unexpected odd epiphany
are what life really meant, you are enshrined
on every hallowed wall my soul can see:
that sudden smile upon a windy street,
the way you held that book like it was gold,
that time you tried so hard to be discreet
but failed because you could not be controlled.

There are a thousand other moments which
all make me feel incomparably rich.
There's no one else has ever so excelled
creating beauty of what I beheld.
When this world's pain is driving me insane,
I just recall you laughing in the rain.

Never Mine To Lose

Lose you? No. You were never mine to lose.
I'm simply not the one you chose to choose.
I love you when I like you, and when not;
My passion is a land that time forgot.
You're not replaceable. I've tried, Lord knows,
to distance you; to alter or reprove
my heart, in futile efforts to improve
my life. But those goodbyes become hellos.

It doesn't matter what you do, I'll stay
right here. You are my prayer, and I will pray.
However costly, I will pay the cost
of watching you till all my sight is lost.
I have sought others, but to no avail.
I guess that's what they mean by holy grail.

PARADOX

Her laughter hides a stream of savage grief;

beneath her raging runs a river of

a secret joy, a reassured relief.

Her bursts of fury mutate into love.

As individuals and as a pair,

she knows our worth, but won't believe it's true.

The world which we inhabit is both new

and timeless; but to her, it's most unfair.

She's paradox, yet all I need of bliss.

She can be difficult. But I would miss

the blaze behind her eyes, the stunning kiss,

the sense if there's a heaven, it is this.

She breaks my heart while comforting my soul

and shatters me as she makes sure I'm whole.

THIS CAN BE HELL

True enough, this can be hell. But for me,
it's the best kind of hell I could be in.
There are duller heavens where I could be;
but that would be unoriginal sin.
You wear me down, and out. It's no surprise
when you have motives that I can't surmise.
Your manner's rarely rational or mild;
yet you can effortlessly drive me wild.

So yes, I'll stay around. Where should I go
that's likely to in any fashion hit
me with this kind of force? I do not know
who else could make me feel so passionate.
So let the harps of heaven trill the names
of other men. I'll settle for the flames.

Why Horses Run

The passion has not disappeared; it falls
as does the summer rain. With fears
its message might get lost, my soul still calls
for longer life with fewer burning tears.
That doesn't much affect what I might do.
Like horses on the track, I'll simply run
for pleasure, satisfaction and for fun,
remain the same until the race is through.

I think of you each day, that's true;
it's from you that I take my every cue.
You give me reason to desire and care;
you make me want to find a way to share.
Though life remains a mystery to me
It's one I welcome when it's you I see.

THE ROAD NOT YET TAKEN

There's no one brings such happiness as you.

There's precious few can make such little sense.

I want you every time I say we're through.

You bring me ecstasy. You make me tense.

Each time we meet, we realize why we should;

then we agree that we will speak no more.

We say it constantly. We wish we could

embrace, yet stay away, from what's in store.

This could be hell, I know that well enough;

yet heaven's nowhere else that I have been.

The path we'd travel might be dark and rough;

but it's the one I want, from what I've seen.

You offer terror, and profoundest bliss.

The world could disappear. It's you I'd miss.

A Message To God's Messengers

What if there is no plan, no grand design,
no pattern that explains the whole damn thing?
What if the arbitrary lack of rhyme
is all the revelation life will bring?
In these religions that insist they're true,
which worship ignorance and fear what's new,
the fundamentalists who speak for God
are lunatics, or fools, or just plain odd.

Why do we need to justify our days
as though required to understand this maze,
provide an answer for its every turn
when it's enough to live and love and learn?
Just entertain yourself to heart's content;
we're here, regardless whether we were sent.

A Sinner Addresses Those Who Condemn Him

Your way, you say, is absolutely right.

Those slow to understand must comprehend

their wayward souls would soon be on the mend

if they would only, like you, see the light.

It's true that I'm no better than I am,

so greedy for that extra spoon of jam;

a human who slips all too easily,

and covets far too many things I see.

I doubt, though, that you are a different breed.

You speak to God, you say, and he replies.

He spoke to me today; I will concede

that you are in for quite a big surprise.

You always say God knows you are his kind.

He said to tell you that he's changed his mind.

Forget You?

You said, "Do not forget me." Think I could?
It's far more likely that my right hand would
forget my left. You've caused too many nights
of bliss, and some of agonizing strain;
those unforgettable delights, the fights
that sometimes left me half insane with pain.
I say I don't and then I feel I do.
I know no way to not remember you.

You've been the high and low points of my life.
I've soared or sunk according to your will.
Your eyes or words can heal, or be a knife
that slices as we watch my heart's blood spill.
It's quite impossible to forget you.
I can't add one to one and not get two.

Just Be Here Now

She looked at me and said, "Just be here now."
And so I was, and am, and mean to be.
We both know she's unlikely to allow
imagined bliss to rule reality.
This moment's what I'm here for, where I stay.
Her every gesture makes me feel at ease.
Her presence is the weather of today
and I am soothed by every passing breeze.

There is no hour I do not see her face,
yet I stay constant in the role I play.
I lock this passion in its proper place;
that is her need, and so, that is my way.
Each night, I greet the ache that is my heart.
I keep it to myself. That is my art.

Magic Act

It's magic when they don't know how it's done.

You take a bow, then conjure up your twin.

The two of you appear, instead of one.

Is this illusion, mystery or sin?

I've seen you both, but don't know which I know.

If you would share your secrets, I could guess.

But now, I'm lost whichever way I go;

each time I reach for more, I gather less.

Could you combine, or sunder me as well?

Will showing my reflection make me whole?

When there are no more hidden truths to tell,

will we be part of one immortal soul?

The final magic act will be quite clear.

What I can't tell, is what will then appear.

Each day might be my last, I'm well aware.
When the sun rises, I just stop and stare,
my sense of wonder no less than intact
while marveling at fantasy or fact.
I know how brutal life can often be –
irrational, absurd, insane, unkind –
that's true enough for you and yes, for me;
there's no need to deny it. Just don't mind.

Someone invented shoes, hats, glue, Febreze;
imagination's there for us to use.
Each day that dawns could bring us what we please;
Life's what we make of it, and what we choose.
Why should we dance through days with less than glee
at how amazing is that oaken tree?

MERMAID

Her deep green glance scales my finless body.
Suddenly, I am submerged in her ocean,
in this strange glowing world of rhapsody,
of shimmering, mesmerizing motion.
Born without gills or clues, I do not know
how to survive these depths, the liquid flow.
How can I breathe down here, so far below?
Yet I know there is nowhere else to go.

I cannot be without her. What's the point?
I will not leave, nor will I drown. I may
swim within this sea forever. Anoint
me lover, fool incarnate, clown. I'll stay
and cheerfully renounce surface order.
Instead, I'll learn to live under water.

ALL MY LABOURS

All my labours are of love. There's a cost
to that; so many keen desires are lost
to wistful dreams or in translation. Still,
those are the choices of my own free will.
If hungering for praise had been my bent,
or seeking fortune had seemed paramount,
I would have gone wherever I was sent
or found a different means by which to count.

So I've disregarded what many think
I should have sought. I've teetered on the brink
so often that it feels like home. And yet
each dawn that greets me is a life reset.
Love can be misconstrued like a haiku.
But it eclipses all that isn't you.

Role Models

I've read of Jonah's whale and Job's distress.
Those men had little luck with happiness.
Nor did Achilles on the Trojan shore
or Midas, who had always wanted more.
The models whom we tend to emulate
have destinies to which we can relate.
But they pay such a terrifying toll
before they ever reach their dreamed-of goal.

So why choose them to mimic and pursue?
What's wrong with that guy there, or me, or you?
Why be in such a hurry to proceed
along a path unlikely to succeed?
No matter how we wish upon a star,
we can't be anyone but whom we are.

Divinity

First, tell me about God. As you conceive
the implications of the word. Then speak
of what the mediocre and the meek,
the just and unjust, should, or do, receive.
We try to love what we don't understand.
You know what's going on? Has this been planned?
Is there a map for where this path may lead?
Are choices we make free, or are they need?

Yet who on us a blessing will bestow?
Not the panther, who prowls and does not care;
nor the sleek fish that swims through river's flow,
nor anyone indifferent to what's fair.
Our God, and we his image, share this trait:
Each one is the creation each creates.

Blaming Eve

It's Eve we always blame for apple bites,
but how inevitable was that day?
The yearning that we feel for knowledge lights
our way, illuminating what we say.
She listened to the serpent, that is true;
but what else was the girl supposed to do?
That snake was placed there by her trusted God;
and though it lied, its presence was not odd.

If it had offered raisins, or a pear,
would she still be the scapegirl for our blues?
We are aware of ways in which we err,
but that's not Evie's fault; it's what we choose.
Don't tell me, then, that ignorance is bliss.
I'd rather know the meaning of a kiss.

Believer

Battalions arrive softly every day;

those are my prayers, which do not ever cease,

that never fail to light my wended way

and offer such profoundly sweet release.

There is redemption in those moments when

a love suffuses me that feels divine;

however weak the power of my pen,

the praise I offer is sincerely mine.

My Lord laughs with me when I smile at him,

and urges me to joke with those who mock.

He fills my cup up to its very brim.

He is my savior. He is my rock.

When darkest hour begets desperate plea,

His mercy's not a mystery to me.

My Faith Is Flawed

My faith is flawed. When some believers tell
me that their views are blessed from high above,
abusing others with their holy love,
I do not choose to live where they would dwell.
So much around me, I don't understand;
what's going on, what's random, what seems planned.
I try to sense which godhead, person, book
warrants discarding, or another look.

Perhaps there is no deity to care;
sometimes it seems this dance is largely chance.
We strive to make our lives a true romance
despite our sense existence is unfair.
I'm grateful, though, whatever debt is due;
for God created death, but also you.

Angel

What good are wings unless they soar in flight?
Divinity is just a metaphor.
There is no secret passage, hidden light,
Or password that will open heaven's door.
You look to me for answers and designs,
Instructions that will show you every turn.
But if you truly want your stars aligned
Don't covet my wings. You'd just crash and burn.

Go seek your own angelic enterprise.
Your own passions will lift you from the ground.
Your boldest, bravest thoughts will help you rise;
Just have the heart to leave what you have found.
Just fly away; don't worry if you should.
There's plenty known that is not understood.

Sad To Say

You say it's sad to say; yet when you say
it you keep sadness thoroughly at bay.
I laugh at grief because I would not weep,
ignore the pains that make my body ache.
You climb a mountain that can seem so steep,
cannot be certain which path you should take.
We drift through shadows that are bleak critique,
yet every word you speak conjures mystique.

The sun that lights our way sears us as well;
its rays burn as they warm, in paradox.
We hear our music sound in every bell
yet can't escape the ticking of our clocks.
Indifferent life rides over us roughshod;
yet you alone make me believe in God.

CLEARING THE SILL

Sometimes I try to talk to you and find
the words entangled on my thickened tongue
in much the way they were when I was young
and insecure on how to speak my mind.
These days I know a lot of words, yet still
when feelings overwhelm me in a wave
my phrases are elusive to distill;
I don't know which to say and which to save.

So I write sonnets after we've conversed;
if not the best, at least they're not the worst.
I let written locution speak for me
in fourteen lines of hoped-for harmony.
Words may evoke the serpent or the dove.
Know this: mine are synonymous with love.

CLOSE ENOUGH

Though far away, you're gently comforting,

almost as if you hold me in your arms.

Sweet sanctuary's one thing you can bring;

your soothing spirit quiets most alarms.

We're intimate at quite a far remove;

we feel and know what we don't really see.

But there's not much that's left for us to prove;

we're close enough that we can let it be.

Of course I miss you. Every day and night.

I fill the spaces, but it's not the same.

It would be right to have you in my sight.

Still, love is love. There's no one here to blame.

Though distance separating us is far,

we couldn't be too much closer than we are.

Another Life

I may have known you in another life.
I'm not sure how we were involved. Could be
you were my sometime colleague, or my wife.
Regardless when or where or what country,
I am convinced I've met your soul before.
Sometimes a word or just a glance from you
will strike me like a deja-vu encore
familiar while perennially new.

It's not that I am mystical. I'm not.
Romantic, yes; but practical as well.
I use imagination quite a lot,
but this seems real, awareness I can't quell.
Whomever you may be, I know this much:
across dimensions, I can feel your touch.

Asking Us To Dance

You don't know what to say or what to do.
You didn't imagine it would come to this.
You thought it might be fun, just something new;
and then we both experienced that kiss.
Why should we wander, when we see our way,
Aware of all we really need to know?
Let's whirl the night away and greet the day
its endless treasures all lined up in rows.

We're not the first, nor will we be the last
to wonder if the dream is worth the chance.
So let us make a present of the past;
what's gone before is no more than a trance.
Let's join ourselves and redefine romance.
The gods, I think, are asking us to dance.

From A Distance

You love me from a distance, when you do.
That's one way to avoid what might accrue:
an intimacy that is not surreal,
a craving you do not need to conceal.
I know it's safer not to take the chance;
you won't fall down if you don't really dance.
But neither will you know how it can feel
when love is honest, proximate and real.

So stay apart if that's your wish. The choice,
however damaging, is yours to make,
and I will honor it – but not rejoice,
nor pretend to, not even for your sake.
It's sad; but I refuse to be morose
if you need so much distance to be close.

AND YET

And yet…and yet…I simply do not know
how to express my love for you as well
as I would wish. Each time I try to tell
you how I feel, I grope for words to show
how much I'd like to…how to speak what I
can really just express with deepest sigh?
What way is there to adequately say
each molecule that sees you yells "hurray"?

So I write sonnets like a lunatic;
each thought of you inspires another verse.
my brain's a metronome in iambic;
all other tenants of my heart, disperse.
Of all breathtaking poems that I've seen,
you are the one my world most wants to mean.

Time Bows To You

In the end, Time takes us all. But it bows
to you on your way through the circle game;
the aging that will take its toll, allows
your youth to linger. You still look the same.
Some of that is the light behind your eyes
still able to stop traffic and surprise
friends and neighbors with a dazzling array
of fireworks that might make anyone stay.

I know this pleases you. It pleases me.
Your glowing beauty's plain enough to see:
its powerhouse appeal so apparent,
luminosity becomes transparent.
It's true I've loved you deeply, well and long;
but being biased doesn't make me wrong.

I Think Of You

Sometimes, when I grow weary of this world
and wonder if the prize is worth the price,
remember events that left my mind swirled,
reflect that I've done too many things twice;
I think of you, and feel my spirits rise.
All sorts of wrongs are suddenly all right.
The slings and arrows are reduced in size;
appalling day becomes appealing night.

No cause is lost as long as you are near.
The thought of you evokes enormous cheer.
They're fond of torture, but when you appear
my goblins all go out to get a beer.
I think of you, and thank the stars above.
Some call it lucky. I just call it love.

I Know, Believe Me

I know, believe me, what this cannot be.
I've thought about it rather endlessly.
From such as Surrey, with his fringe on top,
to Hardy, whose ardor would never stop,
the sonneteers bemoaned cruel love, and said
they hoped her mind would change when they were read.
They castigated Cupid and their stars
and blamed the moon, astrology and Mars.

There's none of that with which I would agree.
I want you as you don't want me. Yet we
trade love and pleasure, even rhapsody;
a wondrous friendship is no tragedy.
It doesn't matter what we do not do;
there's nothing keeping me from loving you.

Come In, She Said

"Come in," she said, and gave me such a grin
it seemed that heaven's door had let me in.
How could I know, when first we met, how much
she'd mean to me throughout my life? Her touch
transported me; her glance seemed like romance
itself. Through obstacles, through fears and tears,
we have continued all these years this dance
of love, doing what either of us dares.

Now that the end is closer than the start,
I think of all we've had, and all we've missed:
misapprehended acts, bewildered hearts,
made magically well when we have kissed.
Until my rapidly approaching end,
hers is the garden which I choose to tend.

BEACON

You have in you a splendid resplendence.
Regardless how you look or what you do,
your spirit personifies transcendence
no matter which hell you are going through.
So when you worry about silly things
remember how irrelevant they are;
whatever peccadilloes this life brings,
regard them – if you need to – from afar.

When skies are gloomy and then overcast,
you shed light like a lantern in the night.
The future vanishes, as does the past;
our present becomes all that is in sight.
What you can give is much more than a lot.
There might be those would leave you. I will not.

AGELESS

The heart is ardent when it's young. Some think
transmuted time just tumbles by; yet our
passions remain inextricably linked.
When our young blood was hot, we would devour
each hour as if they'd never end. These days,
we hear time's footsteps falling, yet amaze
ourselves with carnal pleasures fulfilling
us in ways still never less than thrilling.

My heart rejoices when my eyes watch you.
The intervening years vanish; you are
the same impossible woman I knew.
I look at you and see my own memoir.
So long as you are willing to be near,
I don't much mind about the fleeing year.

THE SEARCH

I reconsider every aspect of
the life I've led, and live. I don't regret
much, if anything. Looking for true love –
or any love – in those whom I have met
may seem naive, but what else should I do?
Would giving up enchantment be as true?
I know the odds of finding it are slight;
but that's the search about which poets write.

It's not that I don't wish all others well.
I do. I hope they find what makes them kvell.
But seeking fame or fortune's just a bridge
to rapture's simpler, sweeter lineage.
I'd like what people think connotes success.
I'd love what gives me bright-starred happiness.

ALL I ASK

You say that she's not good enough for me,
confiding that you do not see her charm.
You fail to see why she's my fantasy
regarding my attachment with alarm.
The truth is that the woman whom I see
is never less than beautiful to me.
It's in her eyes I daily want to bask.
If she's around, that's all I'd ever ask.

What's love, if not what's cherished most of all?
Why are we here, if not to choose our way?
If we would soar, we cannot fear a fall;
why be concerned about what others say?
It doesn't matter how, or when, or where:
there is no paradise unless she's there.

BASEBALL

Baseball has a magic that can stop time.

They call it a pastime, but if the last

out's not made, you hit forever. Sublime

memories remain in reverse forecast.

Just visualize a pastoral field

of dreams, a fantasy that might well yield

eternal pleasure in a grassy space,

a slice of heaven in an earthly place.

I know those days are gone, not to return,

if ever they were there at all. We learn

to play with all we've got and keep the score.

We have nine innings. We may have no more.

With each pitch that's flung and each swing that's swung

We reach for this myth that helps us feel young.

BATTLEGROUND

You do not solve the problems that I meet,

nor make bad news much easier to greet.

There's often little help that you can be

when times are hard. I'm sure you would agree.

Then why, you wonder, do I covet your

engaging presence in adversity?

Though you can offer solace, that's no cure

for problems that attack successfully.

Yet when I feel you at my side, my strength

is reinforced. The blows that come at me

arrive diminished by the breadth and length

of shield and sword you carry quietly.

So long as you are near me when I fight,

I laugh at all the enemies in sight.

In Any Way, At Any Time

I never thought of you in any way,
at any time, that was not loving in
most every sense. Whatever you might say
or do was where I'd just as soon begin,
and go with you wherever you would choose.
You could be happy, sad or most confused;
when you were bruised, abused or just diffused,
my mission would be banishing your blues.

I've seen you when the light behind your eyes
lit up the galaxy in which we live,
made me consider what I should revise
to prompt you to accept what I would give.
Even when sorrow blends into dismay,
you're reason to anticipate each day.

SEX AND SONNETS

My hands caress the keyboard as they do
the conjured image of imagined you;
the words that flow onto the waiting page
suffuse me with desire to engage
your body and seductive mind. That sex
is of the spirit and the soul as well
as of the flesh does not at all perplex
those of us under its enchanting spell.

So sonnets are the kisses of my night
when you're not here to cherish and to hold;
I write in images of sad delight
my love for you in fourteen lines, controlled.
My sonnets are sex in another way,
caressing you with passionate wordplay.

Capturing Chaos
(for Edna St. Vincent Millay)

She has put chaos into fourteen lines
and kept him there. I read her words: each time
they resonate. Our thoughts align in rhyme.
I follow my own road, but she's left signs.
She stays a light that blazes down the trail
illuminating all my hopes and dreams;
enables me to fight fear I might fail
and helps me reconsider what life means.

There're other guides along my troubled way
abetting me around each curve and turn
who guide me when to leave and where to stay;
but she's the gospel teaching what I learn.
No matter where I travel, she's the star
which constantly assures me where we are.

MILLAY

Her sonnets were the best of all (save Will),
played love's gymnastics with a leaping heart.
Her words, rhapsodic, just would not stand still;
they reshaped chaos into timeless art.
She bathed in passion's endless waterfall,
exulting in the soaking of her soul.
No gorgeous moment was too slight or small
for her; she let them pour into her bowl.

I read her verses now, in love with her,
this beauty who is long dead, true; but not
her rapture, not that consummate amour,
nor all the sonnets that her spirit wrought.
The ardor of her poetry lives on
to greet me every night and every dawn.

AUTHOR

A sailor on linguistic seas that flow
in wavy words which give us cause to pause,
you navigate the tides of thought, and know
when to behave and when to laugh at laws.
You steer your vessel past each dangerous reef,
a trusted guide whose worthiness is clear;
with gentle certainty, you glide past grief,
your calm belief endearing to those near.

Your language is a medicine that heals.
You reach across divides of space and time,
connect with strangers whose severe ordeals
reveal concealed ideals now met with rhyme.
The meanings, sounds and echoes which you write
invite an insight that is lifted light.

AUDITION

This world is whimsical and can be cruel;

frustration sometimes brings us to our knees.

To maintain ideals makes one feel a fool;

we worship far too many gods to please.

Each day's a blind audition, as we try

impressing people we wouldn't want to know;

those smiling faces all too often lie

and leave us wondering where we want to go.

Yet in this urban jungle, there's relief.

Your arms offer protection from outside;

our sanctuary nourishes belief

your warm embrace will make the rest subside.

So let them cry, deny, dissuade and stew.

Our show will triumph with just me and you.

Original Cast

You seemed a miracle when first we met.
As I grew more familiar with your flaws,
I only loved you more for all you let
me share: your preferences, your private laws.
Now that you're older than you used to be,
you're every bit as beautiful to me.
The sorrows of your face simply reflect
the life you live, with which I so connect.

You could go off elsewhere. I know full well
how many other tales there are to tell.
But would we really readily recast
this play we're in, however long it lasts?
Now matter how often we turn the page,
it's you I want here with me on this stage.

JULIET'S LAMENT

Why did you take your life, my reckless love?

Couldn't you have waited just a little more?

Why the sad rush to see what is above,

instead of learning what you had in store?

You could have mourned me without suicide,

but you have blazed a path I'll follow now.

I promised you that I would stay your bride;

your cold embrace is all I will allow.

I wish you'd trusted me to kiss and tell

my plan to you, and not made this our fate;

but your insistence that you die as well

makes my resourceful love arrive too late.

Oh, love, could you not live for me and you,

instead of dying just to prove love true?

IAGO

Don't ask me why. I'm not one who pretends
there is a motive that explains it all.
Do not expect that I will make amends;
I much prefer you kill me, than I crawl.
I don't regret a single false report;
I'm glad that I have led you all astray.
I'm proud of all the havoc that I've wrought;
I wouldn't have had it any other way.

If I'm a devil, you must all be fools;
you trusted me, but that was by your choice.
I ruined you, but played it by your rules;
I see no reason I should not rejoice.
If you still wonder how a soul gets sold,
reflect upon your mirror, and behold.

Puckish

That they are fools, there can be little doubt.
These mortals rarely know what they will do,
or why, or how; but yet, they are about
to redefine a natural state or two.
They're no worse than the rest of us, I guess –
except they think they own the whole domain.
What they consider more, is often less;
they think they're right when they are most insane.

I do take pleasure pulling on their strings;
I laugh when they trip over their ideals.
There's little sense that any of them brings;
they're too concerned with what each thinks and feels.
They rule a world they do not comprehend;
they study what to wear, not how to mend.

READINESS

The readiness is all. So Hamlet said
when contemplating life and what it holds.
There's cuddling, food and drink, and always, bed
to comfort and engage two kindred souls.
There's more cause for delight than for alarm,
whatever fate may promise or portend.
This journey that we're on maintains its charm;
why worry where it goes, or how it ends?

Oh, laugh at the rejections, and the rest;
the hunt for condos, cash and cadillacs.
These quiet, simple pleasures are the best;
you'll have a lot more fun, and you'll relax.
So never mind what is, and what is not.
If this is all there is, it's still a lot.

CELLMATES

The blood flows through the needle in my arm
intended to protect from further harm.
There's irony as it invades my vein
in order for the cells to ebb and wane
so that they can be later reapplied
reorganized so as to interact
with startled cellmates by their pulsing side
transforming theory into instant fact.

The miracles of modern medicine
are marvelous, I know. Yet in my heart
my faith is limited. It feels akin
to magic, less a science than an art.
But whether prayer, vaccine or barking seals,
I stay in favor of whatever heals.

CURRENCY

Success is often measured by the size
of bank accounts, new cars, estates or fame.
The estimate of someone's worth then lies
in how much fashion dresses up their name.
The money buys a lot. The cars are fine.
It's fun to say that this palatial place,
this glamorous celebrity, is mine.
But there are better missions to embrace.

Fear trivial pursuits. Always beware
religions that exclude, or make you join.
Nothing means much if we forget to share
the currency our empathy can coin.
We get most when we realize how to give.
So play your finest part. That's why we live.

DRAGON

I know I am a monster to your race

evoking horror everywhere I turn.

You shudder when you gaze upon my face;

you much prefer me shot, or stabbed, or burned.

You're just as strange to me as I to you

whose skins are shades of tan, not scales green-blue.

Your house holds no more comfort than my lair

in which I breathe my fire as you your air.

You stalk and hunt me. Why? What have I done?

I feed my young, I celebrate, I care.

My outstretched paw is greeted with a gun;

you think I'm queer, when what I am is rare.

The only difference is that I'm not you.

Yet you regard me as you would a Jew.

Earth Sky Star Dirt

My garden in the early morning light
a gentle mist of rain caressing me
so nurturing, provides a lovely sight
of Paradise. It's all I need to see
of Eden, this sweet earth I call my home;
what others see as dirt, I feel as loam.
I love the sky at dawn and in twilight;
I cherish noon and night with deep delight.

A blooming flower always brings me joy,
the blush a small perfection in its lush
display; each plant a friend I can enjoy –
there's nothing in this garden in a rush.
These natural gifts are perfect as they are;
I am enraptured with the morning star.

CAREFREE

I can remember days we were, when all
was new and wonderful, the sky so blue
it seemed a fairy tale, each person true,
each dream too promising to ever fall.
The years brought burdens which would grow and feed,
mutating into hydra's heads, ever
more intricate structures of pain and need,
a mass of bonds one could never sever.

But though the dreams are different now
and disappointments drop like summer rain,
look at this lovely sky, and marvel how
those stars, these friends, raise spirits once again.
No longer free of cares, we nonetheless
create those cares as cause for happiness.

Extra~Ordinary

A little boy stares at some lemonade
as though it were a wonder of the age.
Two teenage girls whisper together, trade
endearments, then continue to engage.
No matter where you look, some marvel lurks
if you just notice that it's standing there.
The world is full of fascinating quirks:
what's ordinary has a secret flair.

We're never short even of oddities;
there's more than we could ever hope to share.
We make and break our doubtful boundaries
embracing what we've been warned to beware.
This life is wonderful in every way
when you're aware that someday is today.

FAVOURITE PLANET

Amazing friends, eccentric strangers, cars
that drive like clouds, food that tastes of heaven,
nighttime skies that smile and wave all their stars;
there'll always be Paris, London, Devon,
Rocky Mountains, rivers, lakes and ocean,
a million marvels that invite our awe;
a child's smile, a thoroughbred in motion --
I'll leave this earth remembering what I saw.

Yet none of these, nor any other thing
are more alluring than you are to me.
Our playful ecstasy makes angels sing;
it's always you I mostly want to see.
There is no planet I'd prefer to this
with all its wonders, and with you to kiss.

Proof Of Something

I didn't believe in heaven till I saw

the way the light played in your hair that day

and felt an overwhelming sense of awe.

Of all the ways I've tried so hard to say

I love you – all those words that disappear

and vanish in the air – none was as clear

as were the waves of love I felt right then;

I knew I was the luckiest of men.

I know that none of this is proof of fate

or destiny or God or anything

but love; yet it is proof of something great

which gives the most unlikely hope new wings.

I can't explain the way it altered me;

but if not heaven, yet it's heavenly.

I've Been In Love Before

I've been in love before, but not like this.

You turn monotony to storied bliss.

It's hard to be concerned with that or this

when offered galaxies in every kiss.

They say that passion does not last, I know.

Well, maybe not for them. But with us, though,

each look, each touch becomes a metaphor

for how what seems so much becomes much more.

I've left you, you've left me. We've tried to make

each other boring for each other's sake.

We've sought for any way to let this fade.

There's hardly an attempt we haven't made.

I'm a romantic fool. But then, you see,

with you there is no other way to be.

IAMBIC

You say my heart beats in iambic. True.

Pentameter aside, it beats for you.

I don't mean it would cease without you, no;

but you provide a place for it to go.

The thought of you inspires poetry

whenever you are near, and when you're not;

I contemplate semi-obsessively

how much I get from this. It's quite a lot.

No matter what, a muse is still a muse;

what has been one becomes, on paper, twos.

There's plenty to inspire and amuse

when there's so much delight from which to choose.

Each time I see you, that's my favorite view

regardless what we may or may not do.

IN ALL MY YEARS

In all my years, there has not been a day
I did not search for love with all my heart.
Too often I have tried to make it stay
when it was less together than apart.
With you, though, the emotion's not the same.
Once you appeared, most everything became
what it now was in reference to you.
Whatever look you gave me was my cue.

So many poems speak of how I feel,
but you have made imagination real.
There's nothing in the world compares to this;
I never knew there was so much to miss.
Sometimes with you, it's all beyond sublime.
My troubles stop. And so, it seems, does time.

I'VE ALWAYS BEEN IN LOVE

Truth is, I've always been in love with love.

I've sought life's meaning with my mind, my heart,

imagination, in the stars above;

But love is where I end and how I start.

I most believe in passion that is grand;

that is the land on which I stake my stand.

Whether spontaneous or planned, such love

is, on my hand, a perfect-fitted glove.

This sonnet's octave contemplates the cause

whose banner has become my *raison d'être*.

The sestet tries to summarize the laws

resulting from whatever fate I've met.

To true love's faith, I take a smiling vow.

In this religion, paradise is now.

I've Never Had A Gift For Giving Up

I've never had a gift for giving up.
When fantasy becomes reality
and what I see is where I long to be
I will not drink from a different cup,
nor will I waver once I've truly faced
what feels so graced it cannot be replaced.
I will not tolerate a lesser dream
when what's esteemed seems to me so supreme.

Will there be obstacles and headaches? Sure.
It's easier to settle for what's there.
But that's no cure for the allure of your
uniqueness, which I so much wish to share.
Let others then surrender or cash in.
That would for me be an immortal sin.

Killing Time

We'll be dust soon enough, I promise you.
We should embrace this passion that we share.
Why spend each night denying what is true,
when we can do whatever we would dare?
Our separate days drift past. When each is done,
we're little wiser than we were before.
We stay unsure what's lost, and what is won;
we sometimes wonder why we're keeping score.

If this didn't last a month, much less a year,
it's still the best creation we could make.
Why then allow ourselves to live in fear
of expectations or of a mistake?
This is a lesson we are slow to learn:
while we kill time, it kills us in return.

Love Song

There're many ways to love. I've tried them all.
Brimming affection, burning passion's call,
pure holy worship, just as whole pure lust,
a tidal wave one simply has to trust –
voracious appetite which always leads
to savage hunger that you need to feed.
The galaxy itself is prone to bow
in universal homage to love's vow.

Yet even in the multitude of ways
I have experienced these passion plays,
when all of them combine they're not as great
as we are in our can't-describe-it state.
So though love has enduringly occurred,
you redefine the meaning of the word.

A Lover Regrets

I have no wish to make you feel so sad;
I like you, more than I can safely say.
But there's no point in doing something mad.
We'd relish it, I know; but we would pay.
If our encounters were much more than brief,
I grant you we would both encounter bliss;
but would it bring emotional relief?
Or would we just find different things to miss?

I pray you'll go away, and hope you'll stay;
I wish I had an answer, or a clue.
The thought of you consumes me anyway;
I live without you, but I know I do.
It's not that I'm unwilling to pretend.
It's just that I won't tear what I can't mend.

You

I wash the dishes, and I think of you.
It's pretty much the same with all I do.
Laundry, watching TV, making the bed,
there's little I hear that you haven't said.
However imposing or slight the task,
I sense you on my shoulder, in my head,
everywhere from the basement to my bed;
I bask in every question that you ask.

It's not that I don't miss you, for I do.
There's not a nuance that I can't construe
into your presence. Ghostly though it be,
the thought of you is all I need to see.
Your whispers to me need not make a sound.
So long as I am breathing, you're around.

Morning Star

You don't keep me from feeling deep despair,
but you can make the pain a lot less real.
Although I carry wounds of what's unfair,
your presence makes it easier to heal.
There's little you can do that alters things
or makes it less exhausting when we care;
but there's a warmth and glow your passion brings
which makes the whole show easier to bear.

So I don't care what obstacles there are
that you, or others, place in our way;
I'd just as soon dismiss the morning star
as leave you if there's any chance to stay.
Sometimes, when fondest dream becomes nightmare,
I write a sonnet just because you're here.

GRAINS OF SAND

We write of life and love and what we feel
at what we see, expressing things we do
not comprehend no matter how we try.
Reality so often seems surreal,
a purple haze turned into green or blue.
We speculate, but really don't know why.
Whoever tells you that they understand
this universe is counting grains of sand.

Which doesn't mean that we need to restrain
our whimsical enthusiastic glee
at what life offers us, however plain
or convoluted it may seem to be.
We may not know the meaning of it all
yet we can celebrate before we fall.

CARPE DIEM

I don't accept my life is done. Should I?
It may be midnight, but it feels like noon.
I greet each day with far more than a sigh;
I know I've got to go, but not this soon.
My memories are rich, but present tense
is where I live, and where I plan to thrive.
To carpe diem is what makes most sense;
with every breath I take, I'll stay alive.

So don't grieve for me – or at least not yet.
With every step I take, I'll celebrate
and keep on dancing till my sun has set.
I will abide before I will abate.
Whatever life remains, I welcome now,
and will not question where, or when, or how.

Only Passion

It's only sex, you say; a carnal link.

It's not security or a safe house.

It's only passion – so you say you think –

a dangerous threat that you must still renounce.

This is temptation, not the real thing;

so what if we get dizzy when we kiss?

It's only grief that this can truly bring;

why trust it just because it brings us bliss?

Then why are we so happy when we meet?

Is ecstasy that easy to achieve?

The peak of all the pleasures we repeat

is how we take, and what we both receive.

There's nothing better in this life we live

than to accept what each of us can give.

Pretty As A Picture

She's pretty as a picture. You can stare
and marvel at the talent and the grace.
She'll give you the impression she will care
what happens with your heart. That's not the case.
She'll tempt you to believe she's what she seems,
encourage you to share the way you feel;
she'll nurture thoughtfully your fondest dreams
then leave you with a hurt that may not heal.

Her mirror shows her a persona who,
though not a real person, offers charm;
but that reflection, as it's less than true,
is less than present, and may cause you harm.
So when you see her, best that you beware.
I know she's beautiful; but she's not there.

A Different You

Although I miss you more than I can say,
the you I miss is someone never there;
she's in my fantasy, too far away
for me to feel your absence is unfair.
I love you heart and soul, that much is true.
The woman that I love, though, isn't you.
Perhaps it might have been, or maybe not;
this story has too subtle a subplot.

The person that I meet each time we greet
each other carefully is different from
the one I thought might make complete the sweet
anticipation of romantic balm.
I love you no less than I did before.
But it's a different you that I adore.

Redundant, Huh?

You think that you're redundant, huh? Then so
are sun and moon, and all of lovers' tears;
and oars perched in a boat you need to row,
or starry skies that lost Van Gogh his ears.
You are superfluous as air I breathe;
though not the center of the universe,
you are its foremost citizen. It's worse
when you're not here to celebrate and wreathe.

I'd live without you if I needed to,
but life would not resemble what it is.
The cloudy skies might seem a lot less blue;
the bubbles in champagne would lack their fizz.
I'll never leave you on a distant shelf;
you're as redundant as is life itself.

Rowing

Raising a sail might be more romantic.

A motorboat would be quicker by far.

Running leaves less time to be pedantic.

If there's a hurry, I could drive my car.

Efficiency's a cause I won't enlist;

fulfillment is a more fulfilling goal.

Arrival's not a reason to exist;

I travel for enrichment of my soul.

So, rowing is my favorite way to go.

The oars in rippling water give me rest.

My contemplative senses seem to know

of all the ways to travel, this is best.

Let others chase horizons at great speed.

This rowboat, and yourself, is all I need.

Shameless

I'd make amends to this world and to God
if only I believed I really should.
But this world's too ironically odd,
and I would have more faith if God were good.
Ignoring standards that are not my own
I travel shamelessly along my way;
when I depart, I wouldn't want you to say
although he dreamed of flight, he might have flown.

You're not required to join me, or to trust
in journey's end. Just understand I must
do what I will, though you decline to try.
I'll compromise, but will not live a lie.
So when I plunge, I do it to the hilt.
I do believe in love, but not in guilt.

So It Seems

It's true that she is poetry to me;
she's often all that I can clearly see.
This fire that warms me burns bright with a flame
reflecting her and whispering her name.
I think of her and realize I must
adjust to deeper stirrings, greater stakes.
She's one true thing I feel that I can trust,
reality among so many fakes.

I can't conceive of life without her here.
That would be like never reading Shakespeare.
She'll ask for adaptation, I'm aware.
I know there will be problems. I don't care.
She's the epitome to me of dreams
my dreams dream of; or so, at least, it seems.

The Art Of Life

There is no end to what we do not know.
The joke is that we think we understand
so much more than we do. Yes, water's flow
makes mud of dirt; but what about the sand?
Our own humanity confounds us. We
blend science and religion in a way
that makes no sense. All that we think we see
might be illusions that may go or stay.

And yet, we think we own the universe,
control our lives, decide what will or will
not be. Although we often make things worse,
we still must be the kings of every hill.
Why must we rule? Why don't we just embrace
the art of life, its special time and place?

The Meaning Of It All

And what if all the answers that remain
once we have sought, and searched, our mind's expanse,
are neither clear enough to keep us sane,
or offer reason beyond random chance?
Should we subscribe to what we don't believe
and wave a flag about the moral right?
Or cynically insist what we achieve
will make no difference on our final night?

I don't know what God may have had in mind,
or what existence means. I only know
that fascinating mysteries I find
are proof enough of what life can bestow.
Each breath of air is no less than a gift
no matter how the winds may change or shift.

The Memories That I Recall

The memories that I recall may not
be what occurred. The traumas, loves and dreams
retained might be mostly mirage. A lot
of what is real, may not be as it seems.
I relive every passionate embrace,
sensation staying in its conjured space,
as actual as when the soldier swore
he felt his limb, gone missing in the war.

It may be I imagine what is past.
That might not matter. It all went so fast;
each moment, although none of them could last,
remains with me, never to be recast.
I am as life has left me, more or less.
That's all I'll ever know of happiness.

THE ONLY CERTAINTY I HAVE

Sometimes, when you curl up to me in bed,

you seem so vulnerable and so small;

a mystifying book I haven't read,

a hidden room with no protective wall.

I love you in those moments even more

than usual. It's normal to adore

you anyway. But when you let me in

your heart like that, I've little left to win.

Would I prefer the thorns upon your stem

did not so often keep me from your rose?

Admittedly, I'm just like other men

that way. Might I leave you some day? Who knows?

The only certainty I have is this:

You banish troubles with a single kiss.

There's Rue For You

This makes no sense. I know, and I agree.

It is not wise in any way at all.

It's not an inability to see

that turns me from the writing on the wall.

But I would rather seek a holy grail,

believing what I know to be most true,

than quit a dream because it might entail

substantial pain and quite a bit of rue.

If bliss were common, bliss would be the norm

and what is precious would be lightly prized.

Our deep enchantments are not uniform

but they're what fantasies might fantasize.

Others may disapprove, critique, deplore.

I couldn't care less. Love be my metaphor.

THERE'S YOU

My troubles all seem minor when you're near.

When ghosts and goblins flourish, you appear

to banish them, providing sensual balm.

Each haunting shriek just turns into a psalm.

The dreaded fears that prey on me can't cope;

those demons whose voices sounded so strong

become a backup chorus to your song.

You are the very paradigm of hope.

So understand that what it is I feel

cannot be substituted or replaced.

Doubt all you want, but know that this is real;

such passion is too great a thing to waste.

Here is one revelation that is true:

there is the world, and then, for me, there's you.

Some Settling May Occur

When still a child, I dreamed of happiness,
of warmth and comforts poured over my head.
I never thought about settling for less
than all that could be thought and felt and said.
As years went by, I learned to compromise,
preferring half a thing to none at all;
that sometimes truth's not preferable to lies,
that some dreams, when achieved, are prone to pall.

The child that I was then, I am not now
yet he and I remain of single mind;
quite certain what we wanted, but not how,
we wend our way, unsure what we will find.
It's not the compromise that bothers me.
It's being less fulfilled than I would be.

Subjectivity

I try not to be sentimental when

regaling pages with romantic pen,

attempt to be objective as the thought

of you arrives. But though I know I ought

to be impartial, how can I? You are

the atom that I will not split, the far

cry in the distance while I wander lost,

the treasure that is always worth the cost.

The living understand, as do the dead,

that little matters but the love we make;

when days and lovely nights have all but fled,

our passion is the last thing we forsake.

So why should I pretend that I care less

than is the case? I've settled for the best.

SURPASSING

I haven't used that word in quite a while.
Superlatives occur, though, when you're glad,
sad, delectable or madly bad;
you turn my phobic into hopeful phile.
"Extremely" is a word describes you well;
you don't inhibit much except restraint.
What you are feeling it's not hard to tell.
Whatever your convictions, they ain't faint.

The sex makes ecstasy seem pleasantry.
Consuming passion reigns, eclipsing each
abruptly dangerous unseen boundary
you raise to keep fulfillment out of reach.
You drive me nuts, yet still, I choose to stay.
You are surpassing in a wondrous way.

Unwavering

"Unwavering", you called my love. Well, sure.

It's unconditional, and deep, and true.

It's there for you to take; there's always more

just waiting for a chance to dance with you.

Why would it waver? You're a glowing light

behind my eyes, a whisper in my ear,

most beautiful of favored stunning sights,

a whirlwind which can banish lurking fear.

So I'm a rock when you're inclined to lean

and trust support that you so well deserve.

Regardless where you've been or what you've seen,

I still enlist in any cause you serve.

It makes no difference what you need, or when.

I'm by your side. And will abide till then.

WEATHERING THE STORM

The storm has wiped out electricity;
we're now bereft of PCs and TV.
Our customary toys have ceased to be;
we have to stop and think, not merely see.
Technology's convenience casts a spell,
seduces us with comforts unconceived.
But what this new world does, it does too well:
a life we once pursued becomes perceived.

Let's use this dark to find recovered light,
a galaxy within that's been forlorn.
Our deeper, quiet thoughts are right in sight;
a more enlightened soul may be reborn.
So let this storm be blessing, not a curse.
Forget sensations lost. Just read some verse.

Werewolf

For myriad nights I've howled at the moon
berating loves arrived too late or soon;
It seemed so clear to me, though not to them
and all too soon became ad hominem.
More able then to feast than to foretell,
I fantasized sating those I dated,
clasping any chance to feel elated,
climbing the tower while deaf to the bell.

Yet when the grandest passions I have known
envelop me in memorized embrace,
no matter that I breathe my breath alone –
I don't regret a single breakneck chase.
I know full well how reckless I have been
by seeking love without more than within.

What Will Be, Will Be

No matter what it is I do, I still
wonder whether we live by fate's decree.
Is there a should? Perhaps a would? A will
that will just justify itself to me?
Or is the endless mystery of life
its own solution? Is all that we see
a carnival of great ironic strife,
that means no more than: what will be, will be?

Maybe, or maybe not. Does meaning seem
an academic exercise to you?
Our acts define us more than what we deem
ourselves to be. It's what we do, that's true.
We may not know which path is best to take,
but who we are? That choice is ours to make.

When I See Horses

When I see horses, or the morning star,
I write a sonnet and I think of you.
There's not a thing out there – or very few –
that fails to remind me of all you are.
A goofy kitten, in its playful way,
conjures how much fun it is when you stay;
a shady tree, a garden anyplace,
whisper your name and seem to have your face.

So it's no wonder that I walk this earth
and never, ever discover a dearth
of reminders: you're everywhere I look.
On my shelf, you can seem the only book.
You are the flying carpet that can bear
me through the air, above my mortal cares.

Why Worry

It's true, some live for money, love or fame;

some seek a power that's not really there.

They covet things without a trace of shame,

not realizing they don't really care.

So often, when we fantasize a dream,

we hold that dream already in our hand;

Reality is never what it seems,

but we don't have to build our hopes on sand.

So much we know, we do not understand,

but we don't need to, to enjoy this life.

Accept yourself without a reprimand;

it's just as easy to find peace, as strife.

To hell with those who'd make you feel depressed;

delight yourself, and you'll be truly blessed.

A Kiss

I do not know the meaning of it all
or why this one may rise or that one fall.
Embracing all my ignorance, I just
take pleasures where I can. Why let them rust?
Or me? Or you? Or streetcars named Desire?
I'd rather nurture fire than work for hire
(although I don't mind that, so long as pay
rewards what I'd be doing anyway).

My friends light every corner of my life.
I do not wish to part their company.
Although not one of them was ever wife,
well, that's okay; and if not, that was me.
There's little left to do but blow this kiss
with trust it will be taken, not amiss.

HEAVEN'S DOOR

I knock on heaven's door without a key
to an imagined lock I cannot see.
We make our own rules as we do our gods,
create personal planets, stars and skies
as we wish them to be, despite the odds
so many of our truths are likely lies.
When we are most ourselves, we choose to be
reflections of our deepest fantasy.

So when I contemplate the universe
that I create, I see it isn't bad:
a disappointing mess, perhaps; perverse,
but one that could be worse, or even sad.
I worship at my altar every day,
which keeps so many falser gods away.

END DAYS

That time will rush right past us without pause
and leave us marveling how fast it went,
that clinging memories become the cause
for which we live, what life has really meant –
these things we know. Yet we cannot avoid
some mysteries, however they're deployed.
We wrestle with remembrance and regret
approaching end days whispering, "Not yet."

There seems less time each time I look around;
increasingly, the cracks grow in my crown.
Regardless what I've lost and what I've found,
Each morning's sun will fade into sundown.
Still, any life that has you at its core
will leave me smiling, not pining for more.

Exit Signs

You see me suffering, but you would give
succor that mitigates my grief for me.
That changes nothing in this life I live
yet your concern lets me breathe easily.
My nights are numbered, so it seems. But then,
for each of us, we only lack a when.
The end of days seems somehow less a scare
when I am made to feel you truly care.

Mistake me not – I do not want to leave,
nor would I willingly cause you to grieve.
I plan to clasp ironic days to heart,
to finish well each journey I did start.
Whatever I've been given, it's been blessed.
I won't depart just coveting the rest.

You Were The Truth

When I thought I was dying, and my mind
reflected on the manner of my days,
researching all the meaning it could find
in what seemed such an enigmatic haze,
I came to you, and stopped – then realized
I had not stopped at all, just circled round
you in a way where it was you I found.
You were the truth. The rest was compromise.

So now I've been miraculously spared
for who knows how much longer, I will stay
not far away, emotionally paired
with you, not tempted to betray or stray.
As long as I have strength to offer light,
I'm here for you however dark the night.

Til I Am Sent

I'll go when death comes, as I have no choice.
There's so much reason why I'd rather stay;
to keep expressing passions with a voice
persisting till it be taken away.
I still seek miracles, or a reprieve;
whatever keeps me here another day.
I'd do most anything to not yet leave,
to keep holding oblivion at bay.

I know the day will come when I won't wake;
I may not have that many years to share.
I'd like to linger for your own sweet sake;
the loss of you is more than I can bear.
Though many cherished souls already went,
I would not part from you till I am sent.

Dust

I know that dust is not that far away.
I'm closer to the end than to the start.
There's little I can do that will delay
the moment that will stop my beating heart.
The time has fled, as poets said it would;
there's so much more to grasp than I could reach.
If I had been more able; if I could
have learned enough to know enough to teach.

Yet still, I feel so hopeful and amused.
The entertainment never stops; the best
seems always yet to come. I am enthused
awaiting the arrival of the rest.
Each breath I take becomes my favorite one.
I love this life, though I'll be soon undone.

MORTALITY

Mortality improves my poetry.
It's being mortal that is not so great.
I haven't time enough to be carefree
nor would I fixate on approaching fate.
I know how Damocles felt with his sword,
his neck awaiting what it most abhorred;
if it were me, I'd be much more perverse
and till it fell, keep madly writing verse.

I do insist on living in a way
that deifies defiance to the state
we all will reach. You can be sure I'll stay
as long as possible, and still create.
I need no one to tell me that I'll die.
I'm in no hurry, though, to say goodbye.

The Times I Almost Died

The times I almost died, or heard I would –
that car spun uncontrolled around the ice,
those several doctors telling me I should
accept I'd rolled my last successful dice –
affected me. On one hand, I faced my
mortality, a coffin beckoning;
on the other, a newly wistful, wry
survival postponed final reckoning.

I breathe each breath as deeply as I dare.
I love each moment I'm allowed to live.
I tell myself to beware of despair;
that though I don't forget, I may forgive.
My life is newly cherished every day.
Whatever comes will not take that away.

HEARTTHROB

I know my heart will one day cease to be
its beating self. That day will be my last.
Yet I recall that moment in the past
its rhythm changed when you appeared to me.
I always loved life, but you gave me cause
to overlook its brevity and flaws.
You've stopped a lot of things, one of them time,
which paused in wonder as I played with rhyme.

You've never aged for me. I look and see
the beauty that was always there. The key
I have received unlocks the world. At will
you bring the two of us to one standstill.
I do not mourn the time we have misspent
on lesser things. I know what this has meant.

About The Author

M. Z. Ribalow has had 24 of his plays receive some 180 productions worldwide, including at Dublin's Abbey Theatre and numerous times in London and NY. They have won awards in London, New York, and regionally.

He has also won national awards for fiction, his widely published poetry, and musical lyrics; co-written ten children's books; and published articles on sports, music, theatre, literature, film, travel, and chess. He is co-author of three books on sports, and is Director of an award-winning sports website.

Several of his screenplays have been optioned; he was film columnist for The Sciences magazine, and has appeared as a film historian on The Discovery Channel and on special feature documentaries of several DVD releases of classic films including *High Noon* and *Sergeant York*.

M.Z. Ribalow is Artistic Director of New River, which in the past decade has developed some 400 new plays and screenplays, almost half of which have already been produced or optioned worldwide. New River writers have won the Pulitzer Prize, the National Book Award, the National Medal of Arts, the August Wilson Prize and the $100,000 Simonovitch Prize, among numerous other honors. He is Director of The New River Radio Show on Art International Radio, and series editor of the anthologies *Plays from New River* and *Currents: New River Fiction*.

He has directed numerous plays in London and New York, was Joseph Papp's Production Associate at the NY Shakespeare Festival for several years, and founded The American Repertory Company of London.

Meir was co-founder and Vice-President of The Creative Coalition as well as International Arts Coordinator of The Global Forum, where he worked with The Dalai Lama, Robert Redford and Mikhail Gorbachev. He has for 15 years been full-time Artist-in-Residence at Fordham University.

2011, a banner year for Mr. Ribalow, saw the publication of a novel *Peanuts and Crackerjacks*, his fourth published play *Masterpiece*, and a poetry collection *Chasing Ghosts*.

Also By M.Z. Ribalow

Novels
Peanuts and Crackerjacks
Redheaded Blues

Poetry
Sanctuary
Chasing Ghosts
The Time We Have Misspent

Plays
Sundance
Raindance
Shrunken Heads
Masterpiece
Tiger in the Tree

Non-fiction
(co-written with Harold U. Ribalow)
The Jew in American Sports
Jewish Baseball Stars
Great Jewish Chess Champions

Children's Books
(co-written with Kersti Frigell & Annie Shaw)
The Gallavants
(series of ten books)

NeoPoiesis: *a new way of making*

1) in ancient Greece, poiesis referred to the process of making: creation - production - organization - formation - causation

2) a process that can be physical and spiritual, biological and intellectual, artistic and technological, material and teleological, efficient and formal

3) a means of modifying the environment and a method of organizing the self, the making of art and music and poetry, the fashioning of memory and history and philosophy, the construction of perception and expression and reality

4) an independent publisher with a steadfast goal to print and promote outstanding poets, writers and artists that reflect the creative drive and spirit of the new electronic landscape

NeoPoiesisPress.com

www.ingramcontent.com/pod-product-compliance
Lightning Source LLC
LaVergne TN
LVHW091225080426
835509LV00009B/1178